I Forgave the Two Men I Vowed to Kill!

DARRELL TOLBERT PH.D.

The EC Publishing LLC books may be ordered
through booksellers or by contacting:

EC Publishing LLC
116 South Magnolia Ave.
Suite 3, Unit F
Ocala, FL 34471, USA
Direct Line: +1 (352) 644-6538
Fax: +1 (800) 483-1813
http://www.ecpublishingllc.com/

Ordering Information:
Quantity sales. Special discounts are available on quantity purchases by corporations, associations, and others. For
details, contact the publisher at the address above.

Printed in the United States of America

INTRODUCTION

One the greatest impulse inside of us is to get revenge on the person or people who we feel have wronged us or indeed have caused us pain and suffering. Revenge is described as the action of inflicting hurt or harm on someone for an injury or wrong suffered at their hands. It is also described as to inflict hurt and harm on someone for an injury or wrong they did to SOMEONE ELSE! It can also be an act that a person perceives to be harmful to them, by another. Jealousy can be an act that a person perceives as wrong done unto them.

This spirit or act of REVENGE is not a new spirit; it has been around for an estimation of 6,000 years. It is recorded in the Bible that Cain killed his brother Abel over the jealousy that God accepted his brother's sacrifice and rejected his sacrifice. God out of love comes to warn Cain concerning this spirit of jealousy! Remember a warning comes before destruction!

(Genesis 4:5). But unto Cain and his offering he had not respect. And Cain was very wroth, and his countenance fell.

6). And the Lord said unto Cain, Why art thou wroth? And why is thy countenance fallen?

7). If thou doest well, shalt thou not be accepted? And if thou doest not well, SIN LIETH AT THE DOOR. And unto thee shall be his desire, and thou shall rule over him.

Verse 7 in the Hebrew Interlinear Bible gives a greater insight. (Note the following verse is how the original Hebrew text reads. The wording is different) 7). Not if you are doing good to lift up of and if not, you are doing good to the portal sin offering reclining and to you impulse of him and you are ruling in him.

God tells Cain your jealousy over the fact I honored his gift and not yours is opening up a portal in your mind which is a path for the spirit of revenge to enter in and cause you to fall (Reclining) but you must close the portal. Unforgiveness and jealousy opens portals into our heart which gives the kingdom of darkness direct access into your mind to influence you to make an unwise choice. This choice will always go against the will of our Father and causes us great pain and destruction. Cain just like so many of us ignores the warning and the next verse says that while they were in a field that spirit of jealousy and revenge lived in his heart because God favored his brother's gift over his causing him to kill his brother.

I really need to analyze this. Cain probably said to himself if it wasn't for Abel then God would have accepted my sacrifice thus this caused him to feel that his brother had wronged him causing the spirit of revenge to enter into his mind. I am sure someone reading these words can relate. As he watched Abel, he probably thought to himself look at him, he thinks he is better than me because God accepted his gift and rejected mine. The truth is I am sure Abel thought none of those things but a spirit of jealousy will flood your mind with all those negative thoughts.

The problem was not Abel, it was Cain. God did not want an offering consisting of things from his garden. God wanted a blood offering because the blood offering was prophetic and a constant reminder of the promise that God had made to Adam and Eve that one day an innocent lamb which was his son will die for Adam sin thus paying the sin debt freeing all his descendants from that obligation of atonement. Rather than being obedient he decided to give to God what he thought would be best thus causing a competition between the two. I am sure it was one that Abel wasn't even aware of. Many struggles with being wrong and being rejected as a result of their bad choices.

God comes to Cain to inquire about his evil deed of killing his brother and to punish him. Pay close attention to the words of Cain.

Genesis 4:11) And now thou art cursed from the earth, which hath opened her mouth to receive thy brother's blood from thine hand;

12). When thou tillest the ground, it shall not henceforth yield unto thee her strength; a vagabond shalt thou be in the earth.

13). And Cain said unto the Lord, My punishment is greater than I can bear.

14). Behold thou has driven me out this day from the face of the earth and from thy face shall I be hid; and I shall be a fugitive and a vagabond in the earth and it shall come to pass that everyone that findeth me SHALL SLAY ME.

15). And the Lord said unto him, Therefore whosoever slayeth Cain vengeance shall be taken on him sevenfold. And the Lord set a mark upon Cain, lest ANY FINDING HIM SHOULD KILL HIM.

Cain cries to God saying because I have killed my brother others will seek REVENGE and try to kill me for my evil deed. God puts a mark which represents the blood to keep everyone from taking revenge on Cain. During the height of anger and rage taking revenge on a person seems so fulfilling but after the deed is done and the rage and anger is gone now you have to deal with the guilt from your actions.

I was in prison for selling crack cocaine and while incarcerated I ran across a few people who had murdered someone as a result of revenge and was given a life sentence. The one thing they all say is this, If I could rewind the hands of time, I wouldn't have taken revenge! Forever behind those prison fences over something they could have avoided! Forever with the thoughts of should've or could've! The revenge at the moment was sweet but now their life is ruined and the sweetness has turned into a very sour and bitter taste. The SWEETNESS no longer remembered only the SOURNESS.

I Forgave the Two men I Vowed to Kill!

I was raised going to church but like most I went not because it was a heart desire of mine but because I had no choice in the matter. Therefore, I grew up with an awareness that there was a God but I had no relationship with him. I also had more questions than answers, the Bible didn't make sense.

The denomination my father had chosen was Seventh Day Adventist and that made it worse! From sunset Friday night until sunset Saturday night we couldn't talk on the telephone, we couldn't watch television, ride our bikes or do anything fun. I hated it with a passion! The real hate came during my high school year. I was gifted with athletic ability beyond belief. My freshman year we played on Tuesday night so that didn't conflict with the sabbath. We went undefeated that year, I played running back. A perfect 6-0 record. I was awarded the 101% effort Award. In my mind I thought I should have received the best offense back award and I believed they gave me that award because they knew they screwed me over.

My sophomore year I played running back and free Safety; we became the first J.V in our school history to go undefeated.

A perfect 8-0. The Varsity coaches wanted me to play on the Varsity team but they played on Friday nights and my daddy wasn't going to allow me to play because it violated the Sabbath. I was awarded the best defensive back. I wanted to play on the varsity team because I wanted to have a chance at playing in the NFL. Resentments started building up, my eleventh-grade year I played on the J.V team again and we went undefeated again. I was awarded the Most Valuable player. I have a perfect 21-0 record as a football player. Sixteen trophies in various sports football, baseball and basketball.

My twelfth-grade year I didn't play any sports because of the Friday night Sabbath. Now a senior in high school I found myself wondering what I wanted to do with my life. My Daddy had his own masonry business. However, that was not for me! As a kid I went to school Monday through Friday. On Saturday you couldn't do anything but go to church then on Sunday I had to go to work with my Daddy. On spring break when other kids were having fun I was working with my Daddy. Summer breaks the same thing. Construction is hard work however I didn't mind the hard work because that is what made me a great football player. Pushing wheelbarrows full of mud through the soft sand gave me balance and a low center of gravity which helped me tremendously as a running back.

Digging in deep while forcing all your strength into moving forward helped me tremendously as a free safety because when I went to make a tackle, I used the same force to deliver a powerful blow to the person with the ball. However, I hated it because it seemed like there was no time for me to have fun. Also it was so cold out there in the winter time and so hot out there in the summertime. My Daddy expected me and my other three brothers to work in his business forever. Until this very day all three of them have their own construction company. Well, I decided at a young age that type of work would not be my future.

I had a tremendous amount of pressure on me to succeed. My older two brothers were on drugs and my sister Sharon had begged me not to turn out like them. I had a great desire to become a police officer. I also wanted to see other states and countries so I joined the military to fulfill my goals and dreams in life. During my service in the military, I received many medals for different accomplishments. After serving three years and six months in the military I was given an honorable discharge and I came back home with the expectations of becoming a police officer which would have made my parents and sister so proud of me thus sealing my life of success.

When I returned back home crack cocaine was everywhere. My brothers, cousins and friends were either selling crack or smoking it. I couldn't believe what I was seeing. I remember telling my brother you all are crazy for selling that stuff because you are going to jail. I made a great mistake by not going immediately to apply for a job at the police department, by the time I did go I had learned too much about the drug game. I knew all the big dealers. I was asked a series of questions then given a polygraph test that I passed. I was excited my dream was about to come true, I was about to make my parents proud. I received a call to come back two days later.

They put me in a room and two undercover cops came in and one said during your interview it was revealed that you know many drug dealers would you like to give us their names? Immediately I became upset because the guy giving me the polygraph test said whatever we talked about would stay between me, him and the police chief at that time. I now know that was a lie because these detectives clearly stated the information came from my interview a few days ago. One said we know your brother sells drugs. I know you won't want to directly bust him so we will give you a partner and you introduce him to your partner and he will sell the drugs to him and your partner will bust him.

I was only twenty-one years old and I felt deceived! I replied no I can't do that. He then replied I guess you don't want to be police bad enough? I said I guess not if this is how it goes. He replied then you know your way out the door and I said I sure do. I walked out hurt and disappointed because my parents were excited over me getting this job. I have to break the news that it wasn't going to happen. A week later I received a letter in the mail stating we regret to inform you but we cannot hire you due to the fact you failed the polygraph test. I felt instant rage because they were lying! The person giving the test said we are going to take one test but if I feel as if you are lying then we will take two.

I took the first and he said it was good and there was no need to take a second one. Now the letter is saying I failed. Resentments and anger set in immediately! I felt they were blocking me from my dream and the portal opened and hate flowed in. Years later while I was in prison, my counselor told me due to the rejection I took on the mindset that if I CAN'T BE FOR YOU THEN I WILL BE AGAINST YOU! Sad to say a year later the thing that I was against (Drug Dealer) I became. Totally disappointed everyone who believed in me but the resentments had taken over and I was reclining. I had three thousand dollars and I went to a friend of mine to buy a quarter kilo of crack cocaine.

He refused to sell it to me because he knew that wasn't the person I was. He said no I can't allow you to mess up your life like this. He went and told my oldest brother hoping he would talk me out of trying to become a drug dealer. My brother approached me and said I heard you are trying to get into the dope game. Listen, this is not the place for you! I told him what happened at the police department and he said forget about that, go out to the prison and become a correctional officer or anything else but stay out of this. The portal was enlarging itself and I had no power to close it so I persisted until he gave in. I had cleaned and oiled a drug dealer who went by the name of Snake gun and he rewarded me by giving me a long barrel chrome 357 magnum.

Snake was just as deadly as his name! He had shot a few people, the gun he gave me came from a person he had shot then he took his gun. He is now serving a life sentence in prison for killing a man. I crossed paths with him years later in prison. He had changed, He was a devoted Muslim. I felt really sorry for him because life in prison had to be a living hell on earth. I can remember my first day as a drug dealer, I didn't know how to sell drugs. My brother said don't worry about it, the people on drugs will sell it for you. I went to a well-known drug location called Parkside Gardens; it was a name for the projects. I got out of my car which was a Z-28 with my nickname Pretty Boy T across the front windshield. I walked over to the stairs and took a seat on the bottom two.

After about five minutes a guy hooked on crack walked up and said who has some drugs there is a sale over there. I replied I have some! He looked at me and said Pretty Boy stop playing, you don't sell drugs. I said listen I have some crack. He said let me see. I pulled the bag of crack out and he got excited. I gave him the amount of crack he needed for the sale. He returned with my money and became my runner making sales for me. I would reward him by giving him a piece of crack to smoke. In about two hours I had made a thousand dollars. I was hooked! I remember standing up and looking into the sky and saying to myself these words...This is the life! I will never work again! If I knew you could make this kind of money so fast, I would have started selling crack a long time ago! Three years later I would look up at that same sky but different words would come out of my mouth!

When I came home from the military, I went to my former High school to visit my favorite coach. I loved this man. While I was in basic training, he had signs made, then he took all the females in his class outside. He took pictures of them holding up the signs that said Tolbert The Ladies Man! Those pictures boosted my ego. I showed them to all my friends in basic training with me, I told you all I was the ladies' man and here are pictures to prove it! While I was sitting in his class, he was telling his students football stories about me. He always bragged about me! The two years I played for him we had a perfect 16-0 record. I played running back and free safety. When that class was over my favorite cousin Telva walked in and gave me a hug. Later that day I received a phone call from her. She said Cuz I have a friend that likes you and wants to talk to you.

I told her no I already had a girlfriend but she then replied Cuz please do this for me. Against my better judgment I agreed but I said this isn't going to be anything serious because I am bringing my girlfriend from Washington in about five or six months. Later that day I met Benz which is not her real name but for the sake of identity protection I will call her Benz because this is a true story. She was a nice and intelligent young lady. Six months later I moved my girlfriend from Washington to Florida. I was young therefore I didn't think about checking out the neighborhood as far as crime goes. Even though I was a drug dealer I didn't want to move my girlfriend and our one-year-old son into a high crime area. I saw this complex with brand new apartments for rent.

I rented it but I didn't know that at the other end a block or two away was a high traffic drug area. Once we moved in, I discovered it. The drug dealers were making a killing because the area was located in a place that gave drug addicts from different places easy access plus since it was sort of out from the city limits there was a lack of police presence. They were also cheating the white people by charging them more than what the crack was worth. They would sell a ten-dollar piece of crack which was called a dime and sell it for twenty, thirty or forty dollars. They would take a twenty-dollar piece of crack which was called a quarter and sell it for forty, fifty or sixty dollars. Therefore, they were doubling and sometimes tripling their money.

Even though I was a drug dealer I still had morals. I was raised going to church from the age of eight years old therefore I couldn't cheat people out of their money even though the whole transaction was illegal. Also, there were rules to the drug game. The first rule is to never get high off of your own supply, which means do not use the drug that you are selling. The second is do not sell drugs out of your house and the third is do not sell drugs in your own neighborhood. Therefore, even though they were making a lot of money I didn't violate those rules at first. I would sell my drugs on the westside in the hood. I ran my drug dealing, like a business. Which means I calculated that you can lose money on certain investments. That's why I never beat up people for messing up the drugs I gave them to sell for me. I had drug dealing friends who pistol whipped people who messed up the package given to them.

One day when I came home, I observed the woman who lived across the street from me that went by the street name of Hot

Chocolate entertaining a few white people inside of her house. I kept an eye on this until I was certain she was selling drugs out of her house. One day when she was outside, I walked over to her and said I notice you are selling drugs out of your house. You are violating the rules to the game and that's a fast way to get busted. She responded I know what I am doing. I only sell to a few I trust. I walked back to my apartment and knew it would only be a matter of time. Because I was running my operation like a business unknown to me it was bringing me on the drug task force radar. When I made money I immediately purchased more crack. I had it stashed at my parents' home under the dressers. In pockets of suits on the line or wherever else I could hide it.

Believe it or not at times there is a shortage of drugs and since I had drugs stashed for such an occasion many and even the drug task force thought I was bigger than what I was. They thought I was moving a major amount of crack but I wasn't. I was just running it like a business. The drug dealers in my neighborhood were buying crack from me because I sold big dimes and quarters which they were using to sell at a higher price to the white people on drugs at a higher inflated price. However, this helped convince the drug task force that I was the major drug dealer in that area. One day I pulled up to my apartment and there were five police cars to Hot Chocolate's apartment. I stood outside watching and about ten minutes later they brought her out in handcuffs.

I felt sorry for her but I had warned her that this would happen. A few days later I was on the Westside but the money was flowing really slow so I suggested to a friend of mine whose name was Toshay that we'll go to where I lived and see what money was flowing. Once there I brought two chairs from inside and we sat beside the road. I was violating rule number three by selling drugs in the same neighborhood that I lived in. A truck driven by a white man with a little kid in it pulled up to Hot Chocolate's apartment then back out and stopped beside us. I said are you looking for Hot Chocolate? He replied yes, I am. I responded that she was busted a few days ago. He replied I am sorry to hear that but do you have any crack? I was really leery about selling drugs to white people because they are the ones the drug task force uses most of the time to set you up.

However, since he had his son which look around two years old in the truck with him, I knew he wasn't a police because they won't dare bring their kid on a mission to set up drug dealers and I knew he couldn't be a confidential informant because they won't allow him to bring his kid on such a dangerous mission because we were armed with pistols. Taking all that into account I decided it was safe to make the sale. He wanted a quarter; I gave him two dimes. He replied you gave me too much; I replied no that's the right amount. He was shocked, because remember I told you they were being cheated. Later that day he came back again. Two days later there was a knock on my door and there was a young white guy standing there. What do you want I asked? He said my uncle told me about you. He said you have big pieces of crack. I was very uncomfortable with this.

I had already violated rule number three not to sell in your neighborhood and now violation of number two, not to sell drugs out of your house was being challenged. I told him to wait outside then I stepped outside and sold him the drugs. His name was Billy, he came back again and again until finally he became more than just a customer, he became my friend. He would drop by sometimes just to talk. By now I had trusted him enough to allow him inside my house around my girlfriend and son. He would even pick up my son and hold him sometimes. I received a knock on my door again one day and there was a white guy I had never seen before. He said I am looking for some drugs to buy. I replied then you need to go down on the other end because I don't sell drugs!

He went back to his truck and drove off. This was the drug task force first attempt to set me up. He was an undercover officer. This however put me on high alert. I am now on their radar. A few days later I was pulled over for no reason at all. I had drugs and guns in the car. They walked up to the driver's side and I asked, what's the reason for them pulling me over. They said no reason but do you have drugs or any weapons in your car and I replied no then his next response caught me off guard, then you won't mind if we search your car? Since the question caught me off guard, I replied no I don't mind. They asked me to get out of the car and as they were about to search it, I replied hey wait a minute is this a legal search? One replied if you don't want us to search it then we can't search it. I replied, I don't want you to search it. They replied okay then have a nice day.

Once in my car I let out a deep breath of relief because I had dodged a bullet. Later that day while I was visiting my parents my oldest brother called from jail. He asked to speak to me. Once I was on the phone, he said boy you need to slow down they are after you. Did you get pulled over earlier today? I replied yes how do you know? He said the two undercover officers came to the jail today and said we stopped your brother today. We knew he had drugs in the car but he wouldn't let us search it. We are going to get him. I thank him for the warning and I really begin to be paranoid. I started looking for another apartment to move into, far from this one. The funny thing is the only person I was going to tell where I was moving to would be Billy because I trusted him that much.

One day I was approached by one of my friends who sold drugs for me. He had Billy's sister with him. He said tell Pretty Boy (My street name) what you told me. She said beware of my brother because the police are trying to use him to set you up. I was shocked! I couldn't believe it. Later that day when he came over, I had all my guns set out. A 243 rifle, two 30-30 rifles, 9mm pistol, 357 long barrel pistol, 380 pistol, 22 pistol and two shot guns. I said have a seat and he sat down. I said I heard from your sister the police are trying to use you to set me up? He replied she is lying on me; you are my friend so I won't do that to you. I said you see all these guns? The person who set me up will die from one of them but it will be a very slow painful death. I will torture them by shooting them in one leg. Then the other leg, then in one hand then in another hand then in one knee cap then the other knee cap.

I will make them beg me to kill them so they can escape the pain! Do you understand me, Billy? The thing about this is that I wasn't making idle threats. I had a very dangerous side to me. I am passive aggressive; these types of people are very dangerous. I remember this one time when I was around 12 years old our team was about to fight against the gang from the other side of town. Note these were older people in these gangs but I didn't care. I loved to fight and my big brother was well known for his fighting skills and I wanted to be just like him. They were on one side shouting at us and we were shouting at them. My brother had a gun inside of his waist. All of a sudden one of them pulled out a gun and pointed it at us. I snatched the gun from my brother's waistline and pointed it at him and shouted we have a gun too, what do you want to do? My brother immediately snatched the gun out of my hand.

They fired a shot and my brother returned fire and everyone ran for cover. However, it was at that time my brother realized that I had a dangerous side to me. Then the Army brainwash people and turn them into killers. I remember this one drill we had in basic training. We put a bayonet on our weapon and as we stood at attention the drill sergeant yelled what's the spirit of the bayonet soldier and we yelled to kill! What's the spirit of the bayonet soldier and we yelled to kill! He kept asking us until we were worked up into a killing frenzy to kill! To kill! To Kill! Then he yells head butt to the head! We acted like we were hitting the enemy with the butt of our machine gun. We yelled as we did then he yelled stick and move! We pretended we were thrusting the bayonet into our enemy. This drill went on until we were just yelling to kill! To Kill and throwing blows and sticking the air with the bayonet

As I stated this was for the purpose of brainwashing you to kill your enemy but this type of training stays in your mind forever. He assured me that he won't do such a thing. About a week later he said he knew this guy who wanted to buy five thousand dollars' worth of crack and he wanted to bring him over. I declined and said you can get the money from him and I will do the deal with you and you give him the drugs but he will not come anywhere near my apartment. Unknown to me Billy had got into trouble and his father had taken him to the police. They had been doing surveillance on my apartment and they knew he had an inside connection to me. His sister had been right with the information she had told me. The guy Billy wanted to bring over was an undercover cop.

On the Westside one time we had a family hangout at my cousin Maryann's house. We had a huge family. My grandmother had twelve children and her sister also had twelve children. Therefore, we had a huge family and were very close to each other. I was born in that neighborhood and family and friends hung out at that house. One day I saw a stranger hanging out in our spot where we sold drugs. Some knew him but I didn't because he was younger and I had left for the military so I didn't know some of the younger people even though I was only twenty-one at this time. There were a few guys around him and he was showing them something. I walked over to see what was going on and discovered it was a pistol he was showing them. I asked what kind of pistol is that?

He replied a 38 and I was intrigued because I had never seen a 38 automatic before. All 38' s I had seen were revolvers. I asked if I could hold it? He passed the gun to me; I held the gun in my hand not knowing this gun was going to bring me a tremendous amount of pain and hurt my family deeply leaving me fighting guilt for the next thirty years. For the sake of this book, I will call him Curtis, I handed the gun back to Curtis. I found out later he and some other person had broken into the pawn shop and stole that gun and other guns from out of it. One day I was coming down the road in my car and saw Benz walking. I stopped beside her to see how she had been doing and she told me she was in a relationship with Curtis. I congratulated her and went on about my business. My mother called me and said she had some macaroni for me. I stopped by and went home to enjoy it.

I will never forget this day; it was a Sunday evening and I left my apartment for the purpose of going to the movies but I was going to take my mother her bowl back first. This could have been the last time I said goodbye to my girlfriend and my son. I stopped by my cousin MaryAnn house first to see what was going on. When I got out of my car one of my cousins ran over to me and said Benz has been fighting and my other cousin Telva said no she hasn't, she came over and gave me a hug then we walked side by side inside of the house. She explained that Curtis had beat Benz up earlier, I learned her mother had allowed Curtis to move in with them. MaryAnn, Telva and I talked about the situation then I left to go to my parents' home. My mother and I talked for a while and once again this could have been the last time my mother talked to me.

I questioned this decision for a long time. I could have gone on to the movie but I had about thirty minutes to kill so I decided to go back over to Maryann's house which was a major mistake. She lived about three blocks from my parents. I pulled up and went inside and Benz was there sitting on the sofa. We talked for a few minutes and then Telva came inside and said Benz, your mother is outside. Benz began to cry and I walked outside to get into my car. I opened the door then I heard Telva yelling for me. She screamed Darrell help, help, Curtis is back here beating her up. I lifted up my back seat in my car because that's where I kept my guns. I had the 357 long barrel and a 9 mm but I thought to myself I don't need a pistol for him because he is no match for me. Big mistake for not taking one with me.

I went around the house on the right side and Curtis had to leave on the opposite side because when I came around to the back it was only Telva back there helping Benz who was crying, get up off the ground. I have a very strong dislike for men that beat their girlfriends or wives. I immediately became angry. I was going to take my anger out on Curtis, we helped her through the back door and sat her on the sofa then I went outside to find Curtis. I stepped out on the front porch with Telva beside me. I saw Curtis coming from around a car towards me so I immediately looked down at his hands because I knew he had that 38 pistol. Sure, enough there it was in his right hand, he spots me and says is she (Benz) with you now and at the same time I watched his right hand with that gun begin to rise up. From that point on it seemed as if time slowed down so very slowly! Everything seemed as if it was in slow motion.

This medical term explains the reason for this which is called the fight or flight mode: More time for survival. The bodily processes are speeding up relative to the world outside, which makes us feel as if the outside world is slowing down. The mind is focused and we feel alert. This bodily situation increases the chance of survival, when we have to defend ourselves or have to quickly run away from danger. Because the body and mind are in a mode of extreme speed, it seems like what is happening outside in the world then slows down. Because everything seems to slow down in the environment, we see and hear more details of what is happening. This in turn leads to the feeling that the event lasts longer than it actually does.

I was already moving back towards the front door when the first shot rang out, as I stated it all seemed like I was moving in slow motion. I heard another shot then I heard the whistling of the bullet because it came so close to my head, I could hear it whistling as it went by then I heard a thug noise as it hit the person in front of me. I didn't know this at the moment but a young girl had opened the front door and she had Telva's son who was around four months old in her arms. I heard the bullet hit her in the back. I ran into her and knocked her down and rolled over her and back onto my feet. I ran through the back door and jumped over a fence and ran to my parents' house. When I ran through the door, my mother screamed what's going on because I heard the shots.

I replied the negro is trying to kill me! I think the person in front of me was shot. She was clearly upset over this news. Then my baby brother showed up and I asked him if he had a gun because someone was trying to kill me. He didn't have a gun so we went two doors down and tried to get one from our friends over there. They didn't have one either and then we heard the siren of the ambulance and it confirmed my belief that someone had been shot. We jumped in his car and rushed back over to Maryann's house. When we pulled up there were many people screaming and hollering. I ran into the yard and there was Telva covered in blood. I believe the bullet had hit her in the back and came out through her chest. When they put her on the stretcher and folded her arms, they flopped back open. At that point I knew she was dead!

I screamed in pain and tears… she's dead! Someone said no she is not Darrell and I replied yes, she is! That scene was a very traumatic situation for me. It haunted me for years. Then I saw them putting the young girl I heard the bullet hit on another stretcher. I found out later she was paralyzed because the bullet hit her in the spine so they had to pick her up to remove the baby from under her. I ran to my car and grabbed one of my pistols and went to where I knew Curtis lived. I pulled up and jumped out with the gun cursing and holler for him to come out. A woman came out and said he isn't here. What's going on? I shouted he killed my cousin and I am going to kill him when I catch him. He is a dead man! I then rushed to the hospital where it seems like the whole city was up there waiting for the results. All you could hear was crying and all you could see was tears.

Finally, the dreaded news, someone came out and said all those out here for Telva Burton I regret to inform you that she has expired! All you could hear was wailing and screaming and my voice was one of them! That night changed my life forever! I would live the next three decades blaming myself for her death. That night changed my cousin's MaryAnn and her husband Johnny Wayne's life forever because not only had they lost their daughter but now they had to raise her eighteen-month-old daughter and four-month-old son. My two cousins' loss their oldest sister, so much pain! So much pain! That night ripped our hearts out. Death is an appointment we all must meet but murder is a different kind of death. Murder robs you out of what could have been. Murder leaves you angry and full of hate desiring only one thing.

That one thing is called revenge! I was numbed and my head hurt from crying so much. An angry mob was formed and we drove around looking for Curtis. If we found him, he was a dead man! Finally, around 2am I was so emotionally drained I had to go home. When I arrived home, I told Cindy what happened and she held me while I cried. Finally, I drifted off to sleep. When I woke up, I found out the mob had gone to the home of the person who drove Curtis over there and when Curtis was done shooting, he drove him away, therefore as a result of that they shot his mother's house up! My mother called and said a detective informed her that they wanted me to come down to the police station to give a deposition on the shooting. When I arrived, he took me into a small room. He asked is Loretha Tolbert your sister? I replied yes that's my sister. He said she worked with my wife. We think very highly of her.

He said a house was shot up last night. Do you know anything about it? I replied no I was so tired and drained I went home therefore I wasn't a part of that. Tell me exactly what happened last night. I told him the whole story and when I was done, he was clearly upset. He said this is tragic, such a young girl loses her life and another is paralyzed. We will catch him; I replied you better catch him before we do because if we catch him first, he is a dead man! He gave me a very serious look and said in a very stern voice listen to me! Do not mess your life up over him; he is not worth it. Leave this to us. Do you understand me? I gave him a halfhearted yeah but I didn't mean it at all. Not only had Curtis killed my cousin but he had tried to kill me so he was a dead man walking!

I left and went over to MaryAnn home because I knew all my cousins would be there. When I arrived, I was greeted by hugs. My cousins filled me in on the shooting up of Lawerance's mother's home. All of us had guns, we meant business. All of us were drug dealers and we wanted revenge. After hanging over there talking about what had happened and why it happened one of my cousins said I need to go to an Auto Part store. Who wants to ride with me? Three of my cousins jumped into the car and I decided that since we probably won't see Curtis because the police were looking for him, I put my pistol back into my car and jumped in with my cousins. However, there was an Uzzi inside of the car on the floor zipped up in a gun case. When we arrived at the parts store, I remained in the car to catch a little sleep because I was still tired from last night.

When they finally came out one said look at those police, I wonder who they are chasing? I jokingly said let's go see they might be chasing Curtis. They jumped in and we turned down a road and saw a police motorcycle with its flashing lights on. We turned down another road and saw a person running across the field. I said it looked like Curtis running across that field. When the person turned around and looked at us, I shouted that is Curtis! The police are chasing him, let's get him. I unzipped the Uzzi out of the case but I won't say who fired the shots but shots were fired at Curtis because my cousin's death demanded that he died also! Then we saw the police helicopter flying over and more police cars joining the chase so we turned a corner and I said let me out because I want to make sure he gets caught. I jumped out and started running down the road.

A car pulled beside me and hit the brakes, the window came down and it was the same undercover detective I had the interview with earlier that morning. He was sitting on the passenger side; he yelled get in! I jumped in the back and we took off. We arrived at the field where I had seen Curtis running, they had him. His face was full of dirt where he had been slammed into the dirt and he was in handcuffs. The detective opened my door and said get out. They walked Curtis passed me and he asked is that him? I replied yes that's him. Another officer called him over and I saw them both looking towards me. The detective walked back over to me and asked were you in a red car earlier? I said yes, he shook his head and said you tried to kill him, didn't you? Didn't I tell you not to mess your life up over him? I didn't say anything, he then said get out here.

The other officer asked are you letting him go? He replied yes, I am letting him go. I walked off through a crowd that had formed and caught a ride back over to my cousins and when I arrived, I discovered the police pulled over my cousin's car after I jumped out and drew guns on them and arrested all three of them. They were charged with attempted murder on Curtis; the police helicopter had seen the flames from the Uzzi's barrel when the shots were being fired out the window of the car. It made the 6pm news, the news showed the officers with guns on them as they had them get out the car. They were handcuffed and placed into the back of two different police cars. The heading read family members seeking revenge for a murder that took place last night. If I had not jumped out, I would have been arrested also. The family joined together to bond them out. One of my cousins told me when I got out, they drove to my cousin's girlfriend's house and left the Uzzi there.

Later the charges were dropped because there was no gun in the car and neither of them tested positive for gun residue on their hands. The funeral service was packed! My Father did the eulogy, all were deeply hurt over this tragic event. My mother and sister had to escort me to the casket. I held my mother and cried all the way to the casket. I told them I didn't want to see her. My sister said you have to look at her. I was screaming and crying. I can't. I got my cousin killed! I got my cousin killed and it hurts so bad! Once I looked at her, they had to carry me out but not before I promised her that I would kill him! That was a terrible day for my family, truly sad, sad indeed. With Curtis locked up our only hope of revenge was from him being found guilty at the trial. We wanted him to receive the death penalty for what he did. He was charged with murder for Telva's death and attempted murder on me and the young girl he paralyzed.

I had been out all-night selling crack and spending time over to my other girlfriend's apartment. I arrived home around 5am and Cindy told me that our son was sick so I would have to keep him. I took her to work and returned back home. I was tired, I took off my shirt so I could prepare to take a shower, eat, then put my son in the bed with me and go to sleep. However, my plan was interrupted by a phone call from Billy. This was around 9am. When I answered the phone, he said that the guy I told you about still wants that five thousand dollar worth of crack. Do you have it? I replied yes, I have it. He then said are you sure you have that amount? I replied again, didn't I say that I had it. He said OKAY I will be over later with the money.

When I got off the phone my sixth sense started to go off. I replayed the conversation in my mind and the part of him asking me if I am sure I had that amount after I had already told him once that I had it. I thought to myself something isn't right. My feelings were correct because something wasn't right. The police already had three warrants for my arrest for sales of cocaine from three different events in which Billy was wired when he purchased crack from me. The police had him call while they listened in on the conversation because even though they had those warrants they wanted to catch me with a huge amount of drugs to solidify their belief that I was a major drug dealer. Once I confirmed that I had it the ball was set in motion!

They were on their way to bust my house! I was on the edge so I didn't go right to sleep. I waited and kept replaying the conversation in my mind. I kept coming up with the same conclusion. Something wasn't right! I took this bottle out that I had the drugs in and I am glad that I did. Back then the task force had this passion for driving the 5.0 mustangs. In the distance I could hear those engines humming as they came towards my house flying. A major mistake that they made. They wanted to show out and create a show for the other drug boys on the other end of the neighborhood. If they had come in at a normal speed, they would have caught me with the drugs. I was in the bathroom about to take a shower when I heard the engines.

Immediately I knew it was the drug task force and I knew they were coming for me. My suspicion over that phone call was correct and I ran out the bathroom to the front room and looked out the window and there they were. One coming from one way and another coming from another way. I grabbed the bottle with all the drugs in and ran out my back door. Fortunately for me there was a huge wooden privacy fence that separated the apartments from the property of the person who owns the home on the other side. I threw it over the fence and as I was about to run, I remembered my son was inside so I ran back inside and as I was running back up front the front door was kicked in. They entered with guns drawn because their warrant said I was armed and dangerous.

I guess Billy had told them what I said concerning the person who sets me up. He had also told them about all the guns I had. They yelled get down! Get Down! There were two of my guns right beside me so I jumped down immediately because I didn't want to give them any reason to shoot me. They handcuffed me and set me on my sofa and asked where the drugs were? I replied I don't sell drugs so I don't have any. Oh, it's in here and we are going to find it. Then it hit me that they were listening in on that call and they heard me say that I had it, thus the confidence that it was in the apartment and they will find it. My son had been sleeping but all the commotion had woken him up. He walked over to me and grabbed the handcuffs and began trying to pull them off of my wrist. He then started yanking and yanking, I said Pooh (Nick name) stop Daddy is okay. After hearing me say I was okay he stopped. He was around two and a half years old at this time.

They searched and searched but couldn't find anything. They were confused because they heard me confirm twice I had it. One cop then decides to play good cop. He said come with me; he took me into my bedroom so we could be alone. He said look if you work with me, I can work with you. If you tell me where the drugs are then I will put in a good word that can help you get a lighter sentence just work with me. I replied I don't sell drugs so there are no drugs in here. He then replied okay that's the way you want to play this then we will play it that way. I smiled within myself and thought you think I am a fool. Only a fool would tell on themself. I wasn't that fool! He took me back and sat me on the sofa. They asked me if I had someone who could come and get my son.

I gave them my parents phone number and they called. They told my mother they had busted my home for drugs and I was going to the jail house therefore someone needed to come to pick up my son. By this time a huge crowd was gathered outside. I could hear them talking, someone asked if I was inside? Another said his car is here so I think he is inside. They started the process of taking my guns outside in front of the crowd. All of this was for show to send a warning that if you sell drugs this is how we are going to do you when we bust you. They opened the trunk of my car and took out more guns. Finally, after giving up on finding drugs, they said take him to jail. I only had on shorts. They wanted to take me outside with only my shorts on. I said can I put on some shoes and a shirt? One said let him put some shoes on but he doesn't need a shirt.

They didn't want me to put on a shirt because they wanted to humiliate me in front of the crowd. I was their prized trophy because they believed I supplied all the drugs in that area. They took me out in front of the crowd. I held my head up high and won't give them the honor of humiliating me. They put me in the back seat and then I saw my brother's Cadillac driving up. My mother jumped out and ran inside, in her haste she didn't see me in the back seat. My daddy was driving and he got out real slow, as he was about to walk past the car, he looked my way and saw me. He walked over to the window and said are you okay son? I replied yes sir. He then asked they didn't beat you up did they? I replied no sir. At that point I started crying. My daddy was respected in the community, he was a Minister of the gospel. Here I am bringing embarrassment on his name in front of all these people and the only thing he cared about was my safety.

He only cared about the treatment of his son in the hands of the police officers. I was taken down and the next day I was called outside my cell and told my three charges of sales and possession of cocaine had been upgraded to armed sales and possession of cocaine because they found the guns in my house. I thought I was going to get a plea deal of probation or house arrest because I didn't have a prior criminal arrest. When my lawyer came, he said the state has a plea but I advise that you don't take it. I was confused as to why he didn't want me to take a plea deal of house arrest or probation. After all, I was guilty and I wasn't going to fight against it. He said since they found those guns in your house, they upgraded them to arm sales and possession of cocaine which makes them now first-degree felonies.

The plea is for four to five years minimum mandatory no less than four and no more than five years in prison. My heart dropped! I couldn't believe it. I had just got out of the Army less than two years ago with an honorable discharge and no prior criminal record. Little did I know I was just introduced to the injustice in the judicial system in my city. I replied I am not taking that plea, after we talked for a while, I remember going back into my jail cell pod with a heavy heart. I asked who in here has a Bible? It is something about being in a painful situation beyond your ability to rescue yourself that will make you turn to God for help. I didn't understand everything I was reading but I read the Bible every day because I needed God to help me out of this horrible situation. Later the motion of discovery came in and I found out for sure that Billy had set me up.

The rage was flowing! I am going to kill him. He thought I was joking; I am going to take care of him. My oldest sister came to visit me in jail and during the visit she said God told me to tell you to take it to trial. I told my lawyer to file for a speedy trial. Curtis' jury trial finally came and I was taken to the courthouse to testify against him. The courtroom was crowded and I was sure my testimony alone would convict him. I testified and he had two defense lawyers. The woman that cross examines me tried to trip me up and she tried to attack my credibility. Curtis was watching me with a smirk on his face. I wanted to charge the table where he was seated and hit him right in his mouth. If I did it would have set off a great commotion. All of my family would have rushed over to help attack him. I didn't because of that reason and also I didn't want the jury to have a negative opinion of me so I kept my composure.

The trial lasted two or three days. Cindy came to visit me later that day and she had a sad look on her face. I asked what's the problem? She replied they found Curtis not guilty on all charges. I was shocked. How could they find him not guilty? My testimony alone should have convicted him. I said it's okay. They would have only given him life in prison but now he will be set free and we will kill him when we catch him. We will be the judge and jury and our verdict is death!! The day of my trial arrived; they passed around all the guns they had taken out of my apartment to the jury. Billy took the stand and told how he had been wired and came to my house and purchased the crack on three different occasions. If looks could kill, he would have been dead on that witness stand. I knew the jury were watching me watching him therefore I couldn't give him a hard stare.

However, in my mind I kept saying over and over again you are a dead man! My lawyer on cross examination asked him why would he set me up if we were friends? He replied because he sells drugs and messes people's lives up and he deserves to go to prison! In my mind that tape kept playing, you are a dead man! I am going to torture you before I kill you! I took the stand and told a few lies to try and save myself. The prosecutor was upset because she couldn't catch me in a lie. They took me to a waiting cell while the jury deliberated. While waiting I said this out loud, God I have never questioned your existence but if you are real show me your power today and I will never doubt your existence. Immediately that cell began to heat up and it got hot! I knew something was in the cell with me.

The heat could be felt. A scripture in the Bible said that when God came down, he smoked the mountain.

> Exodus 19:18). And mount Sinai was altogether on a smoke, because the Lord descended upon it in FIRE: and the smoke therefore ascended as the smoke of a FURNACE, the whole mount quaked greatly.

God had come down from heaven and was in that cell with me. God didn't tell my sister to tell me to take it to trial because I was innocent. There is a scripture in the Bible that says before any man can come to God, he must first BELIEVE THAT HE EXIST (Hebrew 11:6). God was making it known to me that he was real not because the Bible said so or the preacher said so but because he personally came into that cell and made it known to me because unknown to me my running days were about to be over. About fifteen months later the Holy Ghost was going to start the drawing process and because I now know he exists, I will be drawn. My lawyer came back to the waiting cell and said it's taking so long because there is a hung jury on one of the charges.

Finally, they came and told me we will listen to the charges they have reached a verdict on.

I came out and sat at the table silently praying. Count one was an armed sale and possession of crack cocaine. Count two was a sale and possession of crack cocaine. Count three was the same as count one an armed sale and possession of crack cocaine. I just wanted to beat the weapon charges because they carried the minimal mandatory time in prison. When the verdict was read on count one it was a hung jury. Count two I was found guilty of sale and possession of crack cocaine. Count three I was found guilty of a lesser charge which means I beat the armed sale and was convicted of a sale of crack cocaine. The strange thing about this is count one and three was the same charge under the same conditions. Therefore, if you found me not guilty of an armed sale of cocaine in count three then I should have been found not guilty on count one of an armed sale of cocaine.

Since the jury couldn't reach a verdict on count one the judge told the prosecutor to drop that charge or to retry me on count one. The prosecutor was so upset with the jury for not finding me guilty of armed sale and possession of crack cocaine. She slammed her books on the table and looked at me and said I am going to get you. That possession of powder cocaine charge I have on you I am going to add an armed to that charge also. I replied I will beat that charge so I am not worried about it. Trust me I will deal with the injustice in the judicial system in another book. Up to this point I had never sold any powder cocaine. When they broke into my house, they found a piece of paper in the trash can where I had cut up and prepared a lot of crack cocaine. I was preparing for that sale that Billy had informed me about. The paper had residue on it. I didn't live there by myself so they didn't know who put it in the trash can. At the least the charge should have been a misdemeanor for drug paraphernalia.

Therefore, they had charged me with a fake charge in which I was not guilty of. About two months later they came to me with a plea bargain. If I plead guilty to the armed possession of powder cocaine, they would drop the armed sale and possession of crack cocaine that was hung by the jury during my trial. Then, that would allow me to accept two years of house arrest. I can remember laughing in front of the judge and prosecutor and saying you are trying to be slick! You and I both know I can beat that arm sales of powder charge if I take it to trial. That's why you want me to plead guilty to a charge, I am innocent of. I had heard that people would plead guilty to charges they were innocent of but I didn't believe it until I found myself faced with that situation.

They knew I would plead guilty to it for two reasons. The first one is because they knew I had been in that jail cell for eight months and the number two reason is because they knew that my girlfriends had both given birth to girls less than a month apart during my incarceration and they were gambling that based on those circumstances I would plead to it and I did. Once out I immediately went and purchased a black ski mask. I searched for Billy and it seemed that at all the locations I had just missed him. I also learned that Curtis was hanging out at this drug spot so I scouted that place out looking for a good place I could hide and shoot him without getting caught.

I never got the opportunity to carry out my promise because house arrest hindered my movement but the hate and desire still remained. After doing a year on house arrest, I stopped reporting to my Community Control Officer and a warrant was issued for my arrest. Once I was captured, I thought the house arrest would be terminated but to my horror unknown to me I had a warrant for a sale of cocaine while I was out on house arrest. The plea bargain was ten years in prison as a habitual offender followed by two years house arrest. I was blown away. This was only my second arrest but as I mention the injustice in the judicial system is real. God had allowed me to get into a situation where I would surrender from running from him. I started teaching a Bible study class with Aaron Hamilton in his jail cell. We had Bible study three times a day. I refused to take the plea bargain and went to trial again.

I was guilty but I just couldn't see myself taking that plea bargain so I went to trial taking a shot at freedom. Listen to my next words very carefully when you tell God to let his will be done make sure you really mean it. Many times, we don't really mean it! What we really mean is God you make my will be done. I lost during my trial. I should have been set free. Their witness took the stand and said he lied about getting the drugs from me. I was shouting in my mind! Yes, I am going home because his testimony was the only thing that could convict me. I had told God to let his will be done but I didn't mean it, but I had spoken it and God honored it. Somehow, they still found me guilty but I will address this and the injustice in the Judicial system in another book or a movie.

I went to prison for six years and five months as a habitual offender followed by seven years of habitual probation. While in there I threw myself into studying the Bible through different Bible study courses and enrolling into Bible Academy. My relationship with my Father grew and the Holy Ghost became real to me and my Great Teacher. I received my Minister license while I was in prison because I graduated from United Bible Institute. I also wrote my first book in prison with the title of Why Am I In Prison? I was released on my birthday February 20th 1999. I came out with a new mindset. While I was incarcerated Curtis was serving a twenty year prison sentence for murder. He had won the trial dealing with me and my cousin so I said karma had caught up with him.

He was driving drunk and speeding then lost control of the vehicle and it turned over and crashed into a building. He jumped out and ran but he was seen, I think, by one of my cousins climbing out from behind the steering wheel on the driver's side and running down the road. She testified against him at the trial. After being out for four years a Pastor friend of mine said do you know Billy? At the mention of that name the rage and anger came flooding back. Yes, I know him, he set me up! He replied when I went to teach at the jail today, he was there. He is an inmate and he asked me did I know you? I told him that we are good friends and we do ministry together. He said he wanted to talk to you and apologize to you. I replied well I don't want to talk to him. What I really want to do is kill him.

He replied you are a minister so you need to let that go and forgive him. I replied in anger that man messed my life up and talked trash while testifying against me. I don't want to talk to him! He said pray about it. Later that day the Holy Ghost began to convict my heart. I called Pastor Noble and said give him my cell number. Maybe a month later I received a call from an unknown number. It was Billy, he wanted to meet me at a store. As I was riding to meet him, I was having these visions of shooting him in the knee cap then the hands. I wanted him to feel the pain he had caused me. When I pulled up, there he was! The last time I saw him was over a decade ago. It felt really weird, He had his five-year-old son with him. I smiled within because I knew why he had his son with him.

He didn't know how I would respond at this meeting so he brought his son to de-escalate any negative feelings I may have had. He confirmed this about seventeen years later when he reached out to me again on Facebook. I shook his hand and followed him to the home he was living in. He introduced me to his wife but as I passed one of the rooms I saw something that gave me the impression that he was still smoking crack. We sat in two chairs on the back porch with a Bible between us. He began to apologize and told me how he had gone on a drug binge so his father took him to the police and they threatened to take him to jail if he wouldn't help them bust me. He said he was young and scared so he helped them. I said do you remember what you said on the stand? You were talking trash and that's one of the reasons I was going to kill you! He apologized again and said I was young and didn't know any better.

I could feel the Holy Ghost pulling on my heart. I could allow this divine appointment to set me free or I could choose to remain in bondage. Our Father won't force us to forgive anyone but he will set up situations to set us free, if we yield to the Holy Ghost freedom and forgiveness will come. I yielded to the Holy Ghost and said I shouldn't have been selling drugs because I knew better therefore it's my fault. If I didn't sell drugs then I wouldn't have been arrested. Therefore, I apologize to you for selling you drugs. We stood up and I gave him a hug then we prayed together as I was walking out. He said Darrell can you do me a favor my lights are about to be turned off, can you give me one hundred and fifty dollars to pay the bill. I stopped and all kinds of thoughts ran through my mind.

I thought to myself God you really have a great sense of humor! I can understand forgiving him but using my hard-earned money to pay his light bill has to be a joke! Since I suspected Billy was back on drugs, I pulled the money out and gave it to his wife and walked outside. As I was riding off it seemed like this heavy weight was just released from off of me. I started crying and I raised my hands in the air and shouted I am free! I am free! I am free! (John 8:36). If the son therefore shall make you free, ye shall be free indeed. I am a living witness that this scripture is so true! All the anger and resentment was gone and I could move forward in my relationship with my Father. Let's fast forward to 2021 which makes it around 31 years since the death of Telva. Unknown to me God wasn't finished in The Making Me Free Business.

At this time, I am now Pastoring my own church and MaryAnn Telva's mother is a member of my church. I also had help to lead her father Johnny Wayne to our Heavenly Father and I had the great honor of doing his eulogy. Who would have guessed that God would use the drug dealer that almost was killed that Sunday night to lead Telva's (who lost her life) parents to the Lord. Indeed, our Father works in mysterious ways. After eighteen years of incarceration Curtis was released in 2021 and the buzz around town was what would I do if we came across each other? I used to do Uber just to make some extra money but I hadn't done it in about two years. This one particular Saturday night I had the desire to do Uber that night.

I went downtime where the clubs were because they use Uber to get back and forth from their homes to the clubs. This way they avoid getting a DUI which was smart. When I saw a spot to park, I looked around and saw that Lift was now in town. When I started there wasn't any Lift and very few Uber drivers. Now I realize it has become popular. Normally as soon as I arrived and turned on the app a pickup came up. I sat there for an hour and no pickup and I knew it was because of all the competition in that area. At least that's what I thought the reason was, I decided to go home. Normally when I arrive home, I turn the Uber app off but for some strange reason I decided to leave it on. When I walked inside my wife Kathy said you are home early.

I replied, there's too much competition out there now, my daughter and wife sat beside me and we were just kicking it and relaxing when the Uber alert went off. I said I have a fish on my line and money is calling. I have to go. I grabbed my phone and said I will be back. I knew the address because it was in the area of my job. I worked for FedEx driving semi-trucks pulling the double trailers and this address was to the Chewy business beside it. It was drizzling rain when I pulled up. I saw a woman and two men standing outside in front of the entrance talking. I rolled my window down and said did anyone here call for Uber? The woman replied wait a few minutes. I decided to check and see where I was going to drop the person off.

While I am looking at my phone, I hear a male voice ask should I get in the front or back? I replied, get in the front while still looking at my phone. When they got in and slammed the car door, I turned to see who the passenger was and to my shock I was looking into the face of Curtis. When he realized it was me, he screamed Oh Darrell! It seemed like time stood still and the camera reel of that deadly night began to play. I replied what's up Curtis? As I was driving to the destination it was the most eerie feeling I have ever felt. He was just as uneasy; he was making small talk but I could clearly hear the nervousness in his voice. My mind couldn't really focus on what he was saying because that camera reel was playing.

I was reliving that night all over again and the man responsible was riding beside me in my car. When we reached our destination before he got out, he said Darrell I heard you were a preacher now. I said yes, I am a Pastor. He replied would you do me a favor and pray for me? The man that tried to kill me is now asking me to pray for him. The man I had promised my deceased cousin that I would vindicate her death by killing him is now asking me to pray for him! I replied yes, I will pray for you but my intentions were to do it later but the Holy Ghost said pray for him now. So, I reached out and took his right hand.

The same hand which held the 38 automatic gun that life changing night! The same hand the finger pulled the trigger many times on that night is now in my hand. I prayed a very sincere prayer for him. I felt his pain from the struggles in his life as a result of bad choices, killing two people and crazy as it may sound, I felt love towards him. When I said amen, he thanked me and I drove off. During the drive home the pain hit me and the tears flowed and I said out loud God, you set me up. I now know why I had this strange feeling to keep the app on once I reached my house. Like with Billy he was setting up the opportunity for me to be free by forgiving the man I vowed to kill. I kept saying over and over God, you set me up!

Once I was home, I ran into the bedroom and said Kathy you won't believe what just happened to me. She jumped up in the bed because she could sense in my voice something emotional had happened. I said God set me up! The person I picked up was Curtis! She shouted are you serious? I said yes and I told her the story. The next day I did a Facebook live and told of the experience and even on that I was crying. I received a call from Curtis asking if he left his work badge in my car. I went and searched my car and found it beneath the seat. I called him and told him I had it. He asked if I could meet him at Popeyes and I replied yes. I arrived there first and ordered some food.

When he came in, we shook hands and gave each other a hug. He said have you ordered your food yet? I replied yes. He said oh I was going to pay for it. I gave him his badge then grabbed my food and left feeling free because once again if the Son makes you free then you will be free indeed. I was free indeed blaming myself for so many years for my cousin's death. The guilt rode me heavily because I thought I was the blame but while writing this book my mind locked in on something I was in denial over maybe because my cousin died. The truth is she almost got me killed by calling me back into the yard to help her and Benz. I used to think her death was an accident and that Curtis intent was only to kill me and she took my bullets.

However, the truth is he was mad at her for calling me to help and mad at me also so his intent was to kill the both of us that's why he shot her first. Four days later Curtis was arrested for being in a car that had a pistol in it. My Father set that night up to free me and I now truly hold no ill feelings towards him. I just pray he gets his life together before it's too late. Many are holding on to unforgiveness and on the surface it may seem as if it's justified. Therefore, its hard in those situations like being raped, molested or someone killing your child etc. However, it's not for them it's for you because it's a weight that so easily besets us, it holds us hostage! Stuck in anger and resentments while the majority of the time the person who caused the offense goes on with their life enjoying it.

Also, it's a necessity because there are two very powerful and scary scriptures on this subject.

(Matthew 6:14). For if you forgive other people when they sin against you, your heavenly Father will also forgive you.

15). But if YOU DO NOT FORGIVE OTHERS THEIR SINS, your Father WILL NOT FORGIVE YOUR   SINS.

Father if someone reading this book is struggling to forgive someone including themselves then Holy Ghost, I pray you give them the power and strength to let go and allow you to free them. Comfort those who need healing emotionally and spiritually.

Darrell Tolbert Ph.D. Son of God! L-Jireh Ministries

Ljireh@aol.com phone 352-361-8473

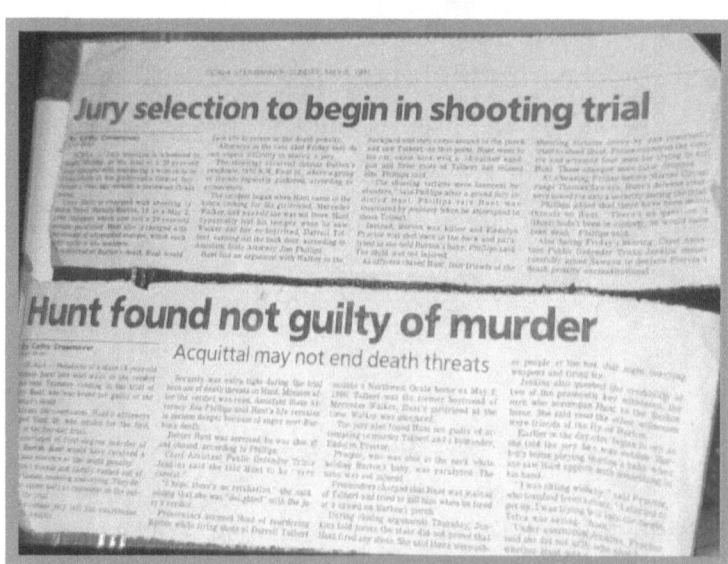

Jury selection to begin in shooting trial

Hunt found not guilty of murder
Acquittal may not end death threats

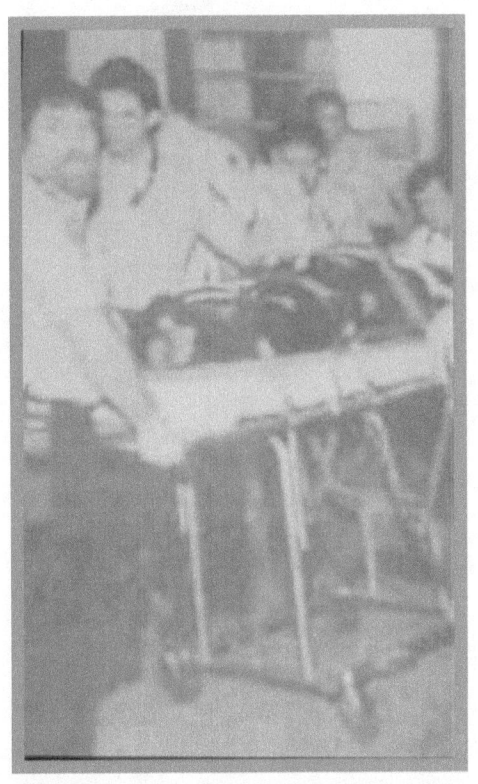

Dr. Darrell Tolbert was born in Ocala, Fl to Wilbert and Lauretta Tolbert. He is a graduate of Forest High School class of 1985. He served three years and five months in the United States Army. He was given an honorable discharge. He is married to Kathy Tolbert, and they have five great-kids. He is a Pastor, Chaplain, and author of seven published books. He is the owner of Cushite Financial Services, V-1 Rotate! Elevate! Motivational Business and L-Jireh Express Trucking. He is also a marriage counselor and a pet Grief counselor. His education includes a master's in divinity, an Honorary Doctorate in Theology, a Doctorate in Divinity, and a Ph.D. in Philosophy in Christian Ministry. He has a podcast show called The Illumination Show with The Doctor, where various topics are discussed. You can reach him for speaking engagements at LJireh@aol.com

www.ingramcontent.com/pod-product-compliance
Lightning Source LLC
Chambersburg PA
CBHW031258120626
46545CB00007B/2875